W9-DAD-700

Sports Idols™

TOM BRADY

Jason Glaser

PowerKiDS press.

New York

To Tom, Heidi, and all the annual Snow Bowlers who brave the Minnesota winter each Super Bowl Sunday to play some football with me

Published in 2008 by The Rosen Publishing Group, Inc.
29 East 21st Street, New York, NY 10010

First Edition

Editor: Amelie von Zumbusch
Book Design: Julio Gil
Photo Researcher: Julio Gil

Photo Credits: Cover, pp. 5, 9, 11, 13, 15, 17, 19, 21 © Getty Images; cover (helmet) © Photodisc; p. 7 © David Drapkin/Getty Images.

Library of Congress Cataloging-in-Publication Data

Glaser, Jason.
   Tom Brady / Jason Glaser. — 1st ed.
       p. cm. — (Sports idols)
   Includes index.
   ISBN 978-1-4042-4184-8 (library binding)
   1. Brady, Tom, 1977– —Juvenile literature. 2. Football players—United States—Biography—Juvenile literature. I. Title.
   GV939.B685G57 2008
   796.332092—dc22
   [B]
                                        2007030768

Manufactured in the United States of America

Contents

Ready to Play

Becoming a football star was not easy for Tom Brady. He had to earn the right to play everywhere he went. Brady watched other people play **quarterback** when he thought he should be playing. He practiced, studied, and worked hard to be ready when his turn to play came around.

Today, Tom Brady has won more than just the chance to play football. He has won the **professional** football **championship**, the Super Bowl, three times. Brady was named the Super Bowl's MVP, or Most **Valuable** Player, twice. He has also gained many fans who think Brady could be among the greatest football players ever.

As the quarterback, Tom Brady directs the team's plays.
He also gets the ball from the center at the start of a play.

A Sports Family

Tom Brady's father is also named Tom. The older Tom Brady and his wife, Galynn, lived in San Mateo, California, with their three daughters, Maureen, Julie, and Nancy. Then, on August 3, 1977, little Tom was born.

The Bradys loved sports. Young Tom's father played basketball, and his mother played tennis. His sisters played soccer and softball. Tom liked baseball and football and played golf with his father. The Bradys were also big fans of the San Francisco 49ers football team. Tom grew up watching the team's quarterback, Joe Montana, play. Tom often dreamed of being as good as Montana.

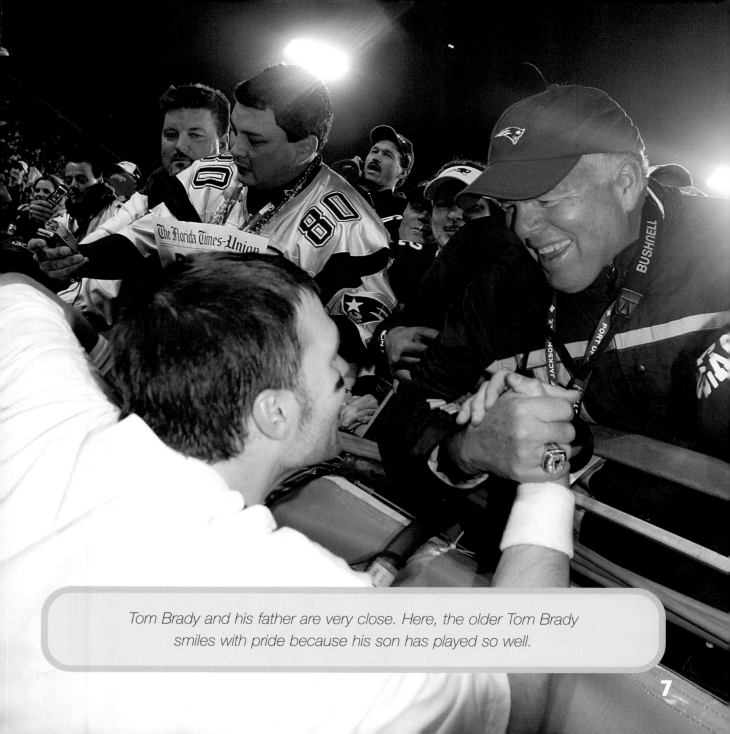

Tom Brady and his father are very close. Here, the older Tom Brady smiles with pride because his son has played so well.

Sharing the Job

In high school, Tom made tapes of himself playing football and sent them to several **universities**. The University of Michigan wanted him most, so Brady went there.

At Michigan, Brady shared game time with other quarterbacks. In 1997, the Michigan team won the championship, but Brady played only four games. The next year, a quarterback from a Michigan high school joined the team. The new quarterback played half the time because it made hometown fans happy. Brady did get to play in some big games, though. In January 1999, the team won the Citrus Bowl. The following year, Brady set passing records to win the Orange Bowl.

Tom Brady helped Michigan win the Citrus Bowl in 1999. He threw a 21-yard pass that let Michigan take the lead and win the game.

The Sixth Round

Brady entered the NFL draft in 2000. In the draft, professional teams pick players who they think will help their teams. Many teams, including the 49ers, did not think Brady could help them. However, some **coaches** for the New England Patriots thought Brady had good football skills. They picked Brady in the sixth round.

Brady showed the coaches that he knew how to pass and lead a team. After the starting quarterback got hurt in 2001, Brady played instead. The Patriots won many games and reached the Super Bowl. Though most sports fans thought they would lose, the Patriots won the 2002 championship!

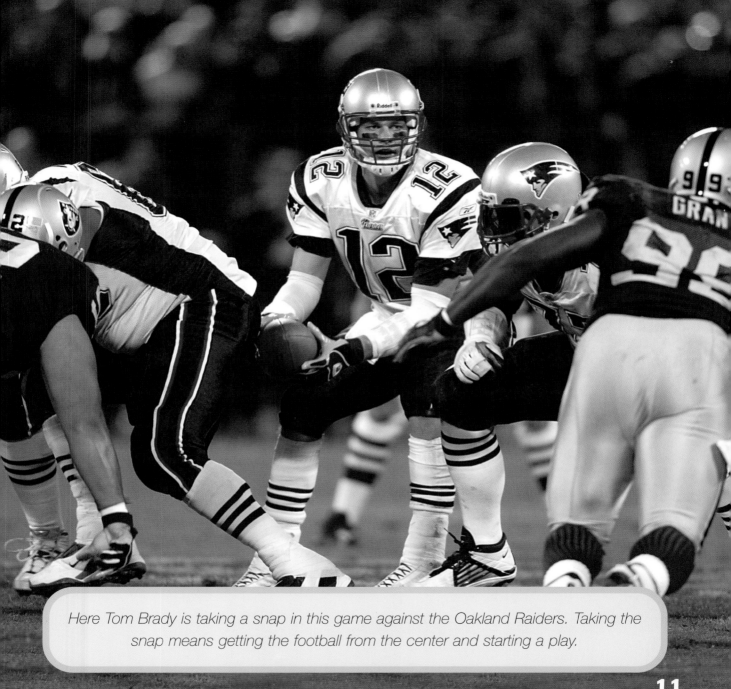

Here Tom Brady is taking a snap in this game against the Oakland Raiders. Taking the snap means getting the football from the center and starting a play.

The next season was full of ups and downs for Brady. He led the **league** in **touchdown passes**, but his passes were **intercepted** 14 times. The Patriots tied for the best record in their division, or group of teams, but did not make the **play-offs**.

In the 2003–2004 season, Brady played some of his best football. The Patriots won 14 of the 16 games they played that year. They ended the season with 12 wins in a row. The team sailed into the Super Bowl again. Once again, Brady led his team to win a close game.

Brady cheered after the Patriots won their second-ever Super Bowl on February 1, 2004. Brady was a member of both winning teams.

The Winning Drive

As the 2004–2005 season started, the Patriots kept winning. They won a record 21 games in a row over two seasons. They made it to the play-offs and the Super Bowl yet again.

In the earlier Super Bowls, the Patriots had been tied late in the game. Brady had moved the team far enough for the kicker to score a **field goal**. In 2005, Brady's plays again got the kicker near enough to score in the game's fourth quarter. The Patriots gained three points and won. Brady became the only player to have three winning Super Bowl **drives** in the fourth quarter.

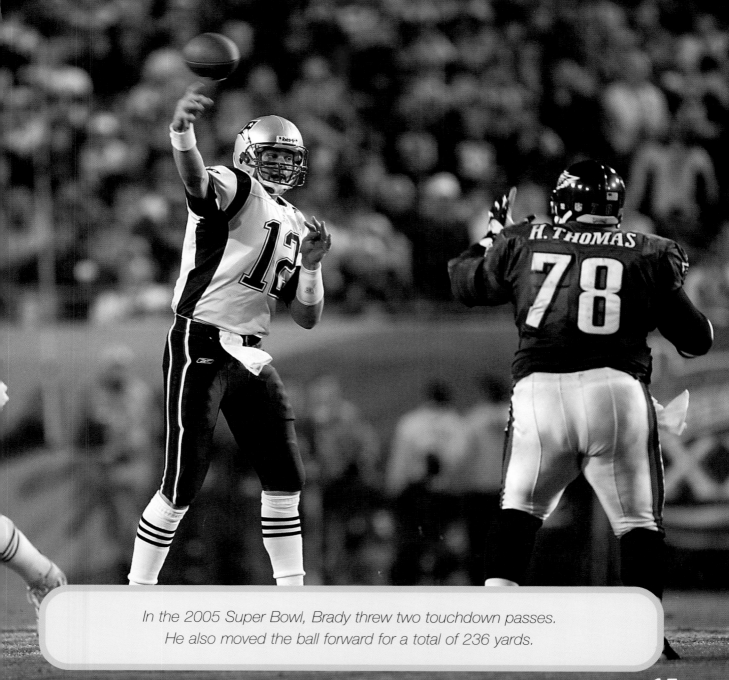

In the 2005 Super Bowl, Brady threw two touchdown passes.
He also moved the ball forward for a total of 236 yards.

More Play-off Chances

The Patriots won three Super Bowls in four years. Other teams worked on beating Brady and his team. In the 2005–2006 season, players from other teams were able to hit and hurt Brady. He was hurt when he reached the play-offs. For the first time since Brady had come to the team, the Patriots lost in the play-offs.

The Patriots got back to the play-offs again in the 2006–2007 season. That year, they made it as far as the AFC championship game. The winner would go to the Super Bowl. Brady played a great game, but the Patriots still lost by four points.

Since the quarterback is the key player on a football team, Brady has become a team leader for the Patriots.

Off the Football Field

Brady likes to spend time with his family. He still plays golf with his father when he can. After Brady started playing for the Patriots, his sisters Nancy and Julie moved to Boston, Massachusetts, to be near him. The Bradys try to spend holidays together whenever they can. In 2007, Tom Brady added to his family with the birth of his first child.

Brady often treats his football team like family, too. Brady likes to play jokes on other Patriots players. He often sprays them with silly string. He likes to play video games with his teammates, too.

Tom Brady likes playing golf with his father. The Bradys are good golfers. They took part in the AT&T Pebble Beach National Pro-Am in 2003.

When he was named Super Bowl MVP in 2002 and 2004, Brady got new cars. Brady gave the car he won in 2004 to his old high school. People bought $365,000 in tickets to win Brady's car. The money went to fix the school's sports building.

Brady surprised a Massachusetts school in 2004. As part of "Take a Player to School Day," he spent time with students during their school day. Brady has visited with football fans around the world. In 2006, he and Patriots owner Robert Kraft visited Israel and watched games played by an Israeli football group.

Tom Brady's football skills have won him lots of fans. Brady makes use of the fact that he is well known to help out good causes.

Becoming the Best

Tom Brady has won every Super Bowl in which he has played. He wants to reach the Super Bowl again, win it again, and maybe be MVP again. He would then have four championships and three MVPs, just as Joe Montana does.

Brady is a lot like Montana. They both throw to the right player at just the right time. Neither of them makes many game mistakes. Once Brady is done playing, they will both likely be in the Hall of Fame. However, Brady is still young, healthy, and good at making players around him play well. Therefore, Brady may even win more championships than Montana did!

Glossary

championship (CHAM-pee-un-ship) Games held to decide the best, or the winner.

coaches (KOHCH-ez) People who direct a team.

drives (DRYVZ) Plays a team makes before scoring points or losing the ball.

field goal (FEELD GOHL) When a football player kicks the ball between the other team's posts. This gets the team three points.

intercepted (in-ter-SEPT-ed) Caught by a player on the other team.

league (LEEG) People, groups, or countries that work together.

play-offs (PLAY-ofs) Games played after the regular season ends to see who will play in the championship game.

professional (pruh-FESH-nul) Having to do with someone who is paid for what he or she does.

quarterback (KWAHR-ter-bak) A football player who directs the team's plays.

touchdown passes (TUCH-down PAS-ez) Passes that let a teammate score by crossing the other team's goal line in football.

universities (yoo-neh-VER-seh-teez) Schools one goes to after high school.

valuable (VAL-yoo-bul) Important, or worth a lot of money.

Index

Web Sites

Due to the changing nature of Internet links, PowerKids Press has developed an online list of Web sites related to the subject of this book. This site is updated regularly. Please use this link to access the list:
www.powerkidslinks.com/sidol/tom/